FIND YOUR WHY

&

START WITH WHY

Workbook

for Individuals

INSTRUCTIONS

This workbook is based on two books: **Start With Why** and **Find Your Why** by **Simon Sinek** and will help you implement the messages of these books:

I. Find your WHY, HOW, and WHAT (where find means to discover, not invent).

II. Start with WHY, which means everything you do – every action you take, every decision you make – should be aligned with your WHY. Starting with WHY not only helps you know which is the right advice for you to follow, but also to know which decisions will put you out of balance.

There are 4 chapters:

1. **WHY discovery for individuals** where you bring together your memories from the past – specific experiences and people in your life that have shaped who you are today. From these stories you identify your themes, choose the one that stands out the most, and use it as a base for your Why Statement.

2. **HOW discovery for individuals** where you narrow the remaining list of themes until you have no more than five, turn them into verbs or actionable statements and write a short description that gives each one some context.

3. **WHAT discovery for individuals** where you think what WHATs are possible – what kind of lifestyle, career choices, and people you surround yourself with – would be aligned with your WHY.

4. **The Celery test for individuals** where you use your WHY as a filter for decision-making. Every action you take, every decision you make should pass the celery test. Use it every day or when you feel important decisions/actions are being made.

First, read the book (if you haven't already) to fully understand why, how, and what... then find your WHY, HOWs and WHATs, and finally, use it as your daily planner/journal (THE CELERY TEST).

WHY, HOW, WHAT

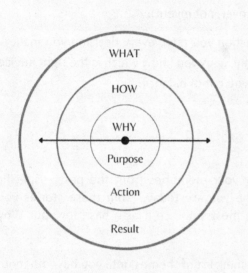

WHY

The purpose, cause, or belief – the driving force behind everything you do. The reason you get out of bed every morning.

HOW

The actions you take (when you are at your natural best) to bring your WHY to life. Personal values and core principles in verbs and action statements.

WHAT

Result of actions – everything you say and do. The tangible manifestation of your WHY, the actual work you do every day.

➢ Communicating your WHY is an essential part of identifying the people in the world who believe what you believe, who will be your trusted friends, loyal clients or customers, dedicated employees, and inspired partners in bringing your WHY to life.

➢ **Everybody** has a WHY. It's not a statement about who you aspire to be; it expresses who you are when you are at your natural best.

➢ Each of us has one WHY and **one WHY only**. It is everlasting and must be relevant in both your personal and professional life.

➢ Through years the words you use may change, but your **WHY will never change**.

➢ The **combination of your WHY and your HOWs** makes you unique and one-of-a-kind.

➢ A **WHY is positive and generative**. It is always in service to others. It makes a positive contribution to their lives.

➢ Family is not a WHY, but a WHAT. Money is not a WHY, but a WHAT.

WHY

DISCOVERY

PROCESS

Your WHY is born from your past experiences; usually is fully formed by your late teens. It is the sum total of the lessons you learned, the experiences you had and the values you adopted while growing up.

To uncover your WHY you must bring together your standout memories – your defining moments – and examine them to find the connections. You're looking for stories that bring to light who you are at your natural best.

What's important is the quality of the memory, the specific details you remember and the strong emotion you feel as you tell the story to someone else.

WHY DISCOVERY PROCESS

1. Find your partner

A second set of eyes and ears to take notes, ask questions and help you interpret your stories. Someone who:

- ☐ genuinely wants to help you.
- ☐ you feel comfortable sharing personal information and feelings.
- ☐ doesn't know you too well (they have a hard time being objective).

Partner:

2. Get your partner up to speed

Explain the basics of The Golden Circle:

- ☐ WHY (purpose), HOW (actions), WHAT (result).
- ☐ WHAT >HOW>WHY vs. WHY>HOW>WHAT.
- ☐ WHAT = neocortex (rational and analytical thoughts, language) vs. WHY = limbic brain (feelings, human behavior, decision making).
- ☐ Achievement (pursue or attain WHAT) vs. Success (being clear in pursuit of WHY you want it).
- ☐ Leader (people have to follow) vs. Leading (people want to follow).
- ☐ Short-term success (focus on WHAT) vs. Long-term success (focus on WHY).
- ☐ Energy (motivates) vs. Charisma (inspires).
- ☐ Happiness (WHAT we do) vs. Fulfillment (WHY we do it).
- ☐ Clarity of WHY, Discipline of HOW, Consistency of WHAT!

3. Pick a time and a place

- ☐ Place where you can concentrate and feel free to share personal stories out loud. Min 2 hours.

Place: **Time:**

4. Gather your stories

Think of at least 5 stories that you consider the most impactful of your life. The more specific you are, the more you'll feel an emotional connection to that memory. And it's this emotional connection that will lead to your WHY.

Think of specific <u>experiences</u> and <u>people</u> in your life that have **shaped who you are** today.

Technique 1: *Peaks and Valleys*

⚲ PEAKS: Above the line put the stories that you consider <u>happy memories</u>: moments you'd enthusiastically relive. The higher you plot the stories above the line, the more fulfilling and positive they were.

♀ VALLEYS: Below the line put the stories that you consider <u>sad memories</u>: events that you wouldn't necessarily want to relive but that impacted your life and shaped who you are today. The lower you plot the stories below the line, the more challenging or difficult they were.

Technique 2: *The Memory Prompt*

What is the earliest, specific, **happy/sad childhood memory** that comes to your mind?

_____   _____
_____   _____
_____   _____
_____   _____
_____   _____
_____   _____

At **school**, what was an **experience you loved/hated**?

_____   _____
_____   _____
_____   _____
_____   _____
_____   _____
_____   _____

What has been a **pivotal moment in your life**, one when you realized nothing would ever be the same?

_____
_____
_____
_____
_____
_____

What happened that **changed the way you think about the world** and your role in it?

_____
_____
_____
_____
_____
_____

What was a time when you **gave of yourself to help someone else**, after which you felt unbelievably good—like you had done something that mattered?

_____
_____
_____
_____
_____

Think of **people** who have been the most **influential** in your life and why – specifics about what they said or did that made such a difference to you.

Who in your life has helped make you the person you are today (coach, mentor, teacher, family member...)?
When they exemplified what you admire most about them (whether they were interacting with you or someone else)?
How did hearing their words or watching their actions make you feel?

_____
_____
_____
_____
_____
_____
_____

Think of **a day at work** when, as you headed home, you might have said to yourself, "**I would have done that for free.**" What happened that day to make you say that?

_____
_____
_____
_____
_____
_____
_____
_____

Think of your **worst day at work** – the kind of day you hope never to go through again. What happened?

_____
_____
_____
_____
_____
_____
_____

What have you accomplished that you're really **proud of**?
Who helped you, who cheered you on, who was waiting for you at the finish line?

_____
_____
_____
_____
_____

5. Share your stories

Share your stories with your partner in as much detail as you can and connect viscerally to your memories and the emotions you experienced at the time.

Partner's job #1: Open-ended questions & *"What is it about ......that ....?"* instead of *"Why...?"*

` How did that make you *feel*?

` *What is it about* this experience *that* you absolutely loved?

` You've probably felt this same feeling before. *What is it about* this story *that* makes it special?

` *How did this* experience *affect you* and who you've become?

` *What was the lesson* from that experience that you still carry with you today?

` Of all the stories you could have shared with me, *what makes this specific one so special* that you chose to tell it?

` (If someone else features prominently in the story): *How did that person make a difference* in your life? *What do you* love or admire about that person*?

` *Describe how this particular feeling* of [*disappointment, helplessness...*] was so *different* that it still comes to mind all these years later.

Partner's job #2: Take notes of the stories and their interpretations in the table below. For each story write "**C**" (contribution) or "**I**" (impact) in the right-hand column to remind you not to move on to the next story until you are clear on what they gave or received (the contribution) and what effect it had on them or others (the impact).

	Factual details of the story	Meaning (interpretation) of the story *(Emotions, feelings…)*	C I
1			
2			
3			
4			
5			

6. Identify your themes

Partner's job #3: From what you wrote, underline/circle/highlight themes, words, phrases, ideas and feelings that recur most often. Then write them in the table below.

	Themes	C / I
Words & Phrases		
Feelings		
Ideas		

* There are no wrong themes. There is no limit to the number of themes your stories may yield. You will need all of them.

With all the themes listed, **circle one or two** that seem bigger than the rest – those that jump off the page. The ones that inspire you or seem to define you and what you care about most.

Partner's job #4: Ask your partner to weigh in on which of the themes seem more important, based on the stories you've told.

Together, choose **one theme** that feels like your unique **contribution** and **one theme** that captures the **impact**.

Contribution theme	
Impact theme	

7. Draft your why

Make the statement:

- ☐ simple and clear,
- ☐ actionable,
- ☐ focused on the effect you'll have on others,
- ☐ expressed in affirmative language that resonates with you.

* Draft is not perfection – only something that feels right.

Your draft

To_____

(The contribution you make to the lives of others)

so that _____.

(The impact of your contribution)

Your partner's draft

To_____

(The contribution you make to the lives of others)

so that _____.

(The impact of your contribution)

Together choose one of these two or combine them:

The final draft of WHY STATEMENT

To_____

(The contribution you make to the lives of others)

so that _____.

(The impact of your contribution)

8. Refine your why statement

The goal of testing and refining your Why Statement isn't to make it sound better, it's to make it **feel** better → When you say: *"That's me – that's who I am!"*

The words don't need to be perfect in order for you to begin to put your statement into practice. As you live with your WHY it will become easier to find the perfect words because you'll be more conscious of your goal and how you're trying to reach it. So take some time to sit with your Why Statement, but don't sit for too long. The reason to find your WHY is so that you can **act on it.**

The tattoo test

Do you like the words in your Why Statement enough to have them tattooed on your body?

☐ YES (Great, go for it!)

☐ NO (You haven't found the words you "love" and relate to yet.)

The Friends test

Make a list of your closest friends – the people who are always there for you, and you there for them:

Friends	
_____	_____
_____	_____
_____	_____

Have a conversation with each of them:

1. First question: *"**Why** are you friends with me?"*
2. Reframe: *"**What is it about me** that made you choose to be friends with me?"*
3. Dig: *"What is it about me **in particular**?"*
4. Dig dipper: *"Yeah, but what **specifically is it about me**?"* (Continue to push them beyond the rational answers.)
5. The answer you are looking for: When they start describing **how you make them feel** and **the difference you make to them.** In other words, your friend is articulating **your unique contribution to their life**.
6. Your reaction you are waiting for: An emotional response to whatever they say (even get goosebumps or choked up) because they have put into words the true value you have in their life.
7. Steps to take next:
    a) If your friends used a ***word or phrase*** that you ***like better*** (it feels right), incorporate those words into your Why Statement.
    b) If your friends brought ***different themes*** to light, that sit better with you than the ones you identified during the Why Discovery, then you and your partner need to get back to work.

9. Share your WHY

The best place to practice is among strangers. When meeting someone for the first time, they almost always ask, "What do you do?" This is your opportunity to **start with WHY**.

When you start with WHY, it **attracts people who believe what you believe** and **repels people who don't.** If a person you shared your WHY with looks at you like you have three heads, it means one of two things:

a) You weren't very clear. What you meant to say and what came out of your mouth were not aligned.

b) Everything came out perfectly but didn't resonate with the person you were talking to. The person who politely ends the conversation or switches topics is probably someone with whom your WHY does not resonate. Remember, the WHY is a filter.

HOW

DISCOVERY

PROCESS

While other individuals may express their WHY in a way that is similar to yours, it's HOW you bring your WHY to life that makes you unique. As a result, the combination of your WHY and HOWs is as exclusively yours as your fingerprint.

*HOWs are not aspirational. They express the ways you **actually behave** – the things you **actually do** – when you are at your best. They are the **actions you can choose to take on a daily basis** to help ensure that you're creating the type of environment in which you thrive.*

*HOWs are the ingredients you need to be at your best. Together, they are your recipe for success – your **strengths**.*

*You can use your HOWs as a **filter** to help ensure that the people you partner with, the projects you take on, and the organizations you choose to work in are aligned with your personal values. It works in reverse too. You can use your HOWs to see if you can find out what's out of alignment.*

(i) HOW DISCOVERY PROCESS

1. Narrow remaining themes

The themes that didn't end up in your Why Statement will serve as the foundation for your HOWs, which will take you from theory to practice.

Take your list of themes and cross out the ones you channeled into your Why Statement. Then narrow the remaining list of themes until you have no more than five.

Remaining 5 themes
1
2
3
4
5

*Look for themes that express similar ideas. Once you identify these overlaps or redundancies, you have two options – keep one and cross out the other or combine them to create a new theme.

2. State your HOWs

Turn themes into HOWs by making them **actionable**. Some of your themes may already be in the form of a verb or action, for the rest (traits, nouns and adjectives), turn them into **verbs or actions**, but don't use *"be"* and *"ing"* verbs (unless necessary).

HOW examples:

- *See the big picture.*
- *Take responsibility.*
- *Explore alternative perspectives.*
- *Tie a bow on it (i.e., if you start something, finish it).*
- *Learn from every experience.*

- *Make it simple.*
- *Get up on the balcony (i.e., see the wider context).*
- *Embrace new ideas.*
- *Build relationships.*
- *Push the boundaries.*

- *Take the unconventional perspective.*
- *Keep it simple.*
- *Silver line it.*
- *Share everything.*
- *Focus on the long term.*

- *Break new ground.*
- *Embrace change.*
- *Learn with a humble mind.*
- *Do what is right.*
- *Work together.*

Examples of HOW formations:

- *Courtesy => Treat people with kindness and respect.*
- *Innovation => Look at the problem from a different angle.*
- *Integrity => Always do the right thing.*

HOWs in a simple, actionable way
Themes in verbs and action statements.

1	
2	
3	
4	
5	

* Make sure the words you use resonate with you and remind you of the stories behind them. It's this emotional connection that will inspire you to put these HOWs into action.

3. Provide context to your HOWs

Strengthen your relationship to your HOWs by writing a short description that gives each one some context and suggests what it might look like in practice. Keep descriptions simple as you can. This additional detail is useful for you and those with whom you collaborate.

Examples of HOWs description:

1. Take the unconventional perspective.	• *See something from a different angle. Open up to doing things a different way.* • *Ask, "Is there another, possibly better, way of doing this?"* • *Try something. If it doesn't work, try something else.*
2. Keep it simple.	• *When things are simple, everyone can understand. If a ten-year-old can understand what you're saying, you're good to go.* • *Simple language and simple ideas are easily understood and easier to execute.*
3. Silver line it.	• *Find something positive in every situation and every person.*
4. Share everything.	• *Share ideas and feelings. Invite and teach others to share too.* • *Share your idea, especially if it's not perfect. Even the "worst" ideas can be built upon.* • *Others won't know how you feel or what you want until you share it.*
5. Focus on the long term.	• *Build something that will outlast every one of us.* • *Focus on momentum and trending more than hitting arbitrary numbers and dates.*

	HOW	HOW in context
1		
2		
3		
4		
5		

WHAT

DISCOVERY

PROCESS

*Authenticity = **balanced Golden Circle**. It means that everything you say and everything you do you actually believe.*

*Copying WHAT other people do or have, or HOW they live their lives probably won't work for you. Even if you copy successful people. It is not just WHAT or HOW you do things that matters, what matters more is that WHAT and HOW you do things is **consistent with your WHY**. Only then will your practices indeed be best. There is nothing inherently wrong with looking to others to learn what they do, the challenge is knowing what practices or advice to follow.*

*WHATs are everything you say and do – they are **tangible proof** of your purpose.*

WHAT DISCOVERY PROCESS

Think of what WHATs are possible, knowing your WHY. Consider 3 WHAT groups:

  a) Lifestyle (diet and exercise, hobbies, personal appearance, possessions...)

  b) Career (job, business, side hustle, projects, volunteer job...)

  c) People (love partner, friends, business partners...)

First, write your Why Statement and your HOWs, then describe what WHATs would be the result of your HOWs and would reflect your WHY.

YOUR LIFESTYLE

YOUR WHY

Why statement *(Your purpose, your belief)*

_____
_____
_____
_____
_____
_____
_____
_____
_____

YOUR HOWs

Actions *(How you do things)*

_____
_____
_____
_____
_____
_____
_____
_____
_____

YOUR WHATs

Result of your actions *(The tangible proof)*

Knowing this is your WHY, what lifestyle would reflect that?

DIET & EXERCISE: _____
_____
_____
_____
_____

HOBBIES: _____
_____
_____
_____
_____

PERSONAL APPEARANCE: _____
_____
_____
_____

POSSESSIONS: _____
_____
_____
_____
_____

YOUR CAREER

YOUR WHY

Why statement *(Your purpose, your belief)*

_____
_____
_____
_____
_____
_____
_____
_____

YOUR HOWs

Actions *(How you do things)*

_____
_____
_____
_____
_____
_____
_____
_____

YOUR WHATs

Result of your actions *(The tangible proof)*

Knowing this is your WHY, what career would reflect that?

BUSINESS: _____
_____
_____
_____

JOB (organization to work for; position in that organization): _____
_____
_____
_____

PROJECTS: _____
_____
_____
_____

SIDE HUSTLE, VOLUNTEER JOB: _____
_____
_____
_____

PEOPLE AROUND YOU

YOUR WHY

Why statement *(Your purpose, your belief)*

_____

_____

_____

_____

_____

_____

_____

_____

_____

YOUR HOWs

Actions *(How you do things)*

_____

_____

_____

_____

_____

_____

_____

_____

_____

YOUR WHATs

Result of your actions *(The tangible proof)*

Knowing this is your WHY, what kind of people would you want in your life?

LOVE PARTNER: _____

_____

_____

_____

_____

FRIENDS: _____

_____

_____

_____

_____

OTHERS (Business partners, Coworkers, Employees, Boss...)

_____

_____

_____

_____

_____

_____

_____

THE

CELERY TEST

JOURNAL

*Once you know your WHY, you have a choice to **live it every day**. Living it means consistently taking actions that are in alignment with the things you say.*

*Once you understand your WHY, you'll be able to clearly articulate **what makes you feel fulfilled** and to better understand **what drives your behavior** when you're at your natural best. When you can do that, you'll have a point of reference (the celery test) for everything you do going forward.*

*You'll be able to make more **intentional choices** for your business, your career and your life. You'll be able to inspire others to buy from you, work with you and join your cause.*

*To keep the WHY alive over time, you must keep it front and center, **communicating** it and **committing** to living it – on purpose, with purpose – every day. Otherwise, a WHY can fizzle, fade, or be forgotten.*

*Your WHY comes from your stories – the moments in your life when you felt most fulfilled, the moments when you were your very best self. The more you **act intentionally on your WHY**, the **more of these stories you will collect**. And those stories will deepen your relationship to your WHY and inspire you to keep going. In turn, you'll inspire others.*

BRING THE WHY TO LIFE IN YOUR DAY-TO-DAY LIFE

A WHY provides a clear **filter** for decision-making. Every decision – lifestyle, career, people – should pass the Celery Test. There are 120 pages of celery test journals; use it every day or when you feel important decisions/actions are being made.

1. First, write your Why statement and your HOWs (to internalize them).

2. Then describe all your decision/actions that **are (were) and aren't (weren't) aligned** with your WHY.

THE CELERY TEST FOR INDIVIDUALS

Date:_____

YOUR WHY	YOUR HOWs
_____	_____
_____	_____
_____	_____
_____	_____
_____	_____
_____	_____
_____	_____
_____	_____

YOUR WHATs

Decisions/actions that **were (would be) aligned** with you WHY:	Decisions/actions that **weren't (wouldn't be) aligned** with your WHY:
_____	_____
_____	_____
_____	_____
_____	_____
_____	_____
_____	_____
_____	_____
_____	_____
_____	_____
_____	_____
_____	_____
_____	_____
_____	_____
_____	_____
_____	_____
_____	_____
_____	_____
_____	_____
_____	_____

THE CELERY TEST FOR INDIVIDUALS

Date:_____

YOUR WHY	YOUR HOWs
_____	_____
_____	_____
_____	_____
_____	_____
_____	_____
_____	_____
_____	_____
_____	_____
_____	_____

YOUR WHATs	
Decisions/actions that **were (would be) aligned** with you WHY:	Decisions/actions that **weren't (wouldn't be) aligned** with your WHY:

THE CELERY TEST FOR INDIVIDUALS

Date:_____

YOUR WHY	YOUR HOWs

YOUR WHATs

Decisions/actions that **were (would be) aligned** with you WHY:	Decisions/actions that **weren't (wouldn't be) aligned** with your WHY:

THE CELERY TEST FOR INDIVIDUALS

Date:_____

YOUR WHY	YOUR HOWs
♥ _____	⚖ _____
_____	_____
_____	_____
_____	_____
_____	_____
_____	_____
_____	_____
_____	_____
_____	_____

YOUR WHATs

Decisions/actions that **were (would be) aligned** with you WHY:	Decisions/actions that **weren't (wouldn't be) aligned** with your WHY:
_____	_____
_____	_____
_____	_____
_____	_____
_____	_____
_____	_____
_____	_____
_____	_____
_____	_____
_____	_____
_____	_____
_____	_____
_____	_____
_____	_____
_____	_____
_____	_____
_____	_____
_____	_____
_____	_____

THE CELERY TEST FOR INDIVIDUALS

Date:_____

YOUR WHY	YOUR HOWs

YOUR WHATs	
Decisions/actions that **were (would be) aligned** with you WHY:	Decisions/actions that **weren't (wouldn't be) aligned** with your WHY:

THE CELERY TEST FOR INDIVIDUALS

Date:_____

YOUR WHY	YOUR HOWs

YOUR WHATs

Decisions/actions that **were (would be) aligned** with you WHY:	Decisions/actions that **weren't (wouldn't be) aligned** with your WHY:

Date:_____

YOUR WHY	YOUR HOWs
_____	_____
_____	_____
_____	_____
_____	_____
_____	_____
_____	_____
_____	_____
_____	_____
_____	_____

YOUR WHATs

Decisions/actions that **were (would be) aligned** with you WHY:	Decisions/actions that **weren't (wouldn't be) aligned** with your WHY:
_____	_____
_____	_____
_____	_____
_____	_____
_____	_____
_____	_____
_____	_____
_____	_____
_____	_____
_____	_____
_____	_____
_____	_____
_____	_____
_____	_____
_____	_____
_____	_____
_____	_____
_____	_____
_____	_____
_____	_____
_____	_____

THE CELERY TEST FOR INDIVIDUALS

Date:_____

YOUR WHY	YOUR HOWs

YOUR WHATs

Decisions/actions that **were (would be) aligned** with you WHY:	Decisions/actions that **weren't (wouldn't be) aligned** with your WHY:

THE CELERY TEST FOR INDIVIDUALS

Date:_____

YOUR WHY	YOUR HOWs

YOUR WHATs

Decisions/actions that **were (would be) aligned** with you WHY:	Decisions/actions that **weren't (wouldn't be) aligned** with your WHY:

Date:_____

YOUR WHY	YOUR HOWs
_____	_____
_____	_____
_____	_____
_____	_____
_____	_____
_____	_____
_____	_____
_____	_____

YOUR WHATs

Decisions/actions that **were (would be) aligned** with you WHY:	Decisions/actions that **weren't (wouldn't be) aligned** with your WHY:
_____	_____
_____	_____
_____	_____
_____	_____
_____	_____
_____	_____
_____	_____
_____	_____
_____	_____
_____	_____
_____	_____
_____	_____
_____	_____
_____	_____
_____	_____
_____	_____
_____	_____
_____	_____
_____	_____
_____	_____

THE CELERY TEST FOR INDIVIDUALS

Date:_____

YOUR WHY	YOUR HOWs
_____	_____
_____	_____
_____	_____
_____	_____
_____	_____
_____	_____
_____	_____
_____	_____
_____	_____

YOUR WHATs

Decisions/actions that **were (would be) aligned** with you WHY:	Decisions/actions that **weren't (wouldn't be) aligned** with your WHY:
_____	_____
_____	_____
_____	_____
_____	_____
_____	_____
_____	_____
_____	_____
_____	_____
_____	_____
_____	_____
_____	_____
_____	_____
_____	_____
_____	_____
_____	_____
_____	_____
_____	_____
_____	_____
_____	_____
_____	_____

THE CELERY TEST FOR INDIVIDUALS

Date:_____

YOUR WHY	YOUR HOWs

YOUR WHATs

Decisions/actions that **were (would be) aligned** with you WHY:	Decisions/actions that **weren't (wouldn't be) aligned** with your WHY:

THE CELERY TEST FOR INDIVIDUALS

Date:_____

YOUR WHY	YOUR HOWs
♥ _____	⚖ _____
_____	_____
_____	_____
_____	_____
_____	_____
_____	_____
_____	_____
_____	_____
_____	_____

YOUR WHATs

Decisions/actions that **were (would be) aligned** with you WHY:	Decisions/actions that **weren't (wouldn't be) aligned** with your WHY:
_____	_____
_____	_____
_____	_____
_____	_____
_____	_____
_____	_____
_____	_____
_____	_____
_____	_____
_____	_____
_____	_____
_____	_____
_____	_____
_____	_____
_____	_____
_____	_____
_____	_____
_____	_____
_____	_____
_____	_____

Date:_____

YOUR WHY	YOUR HOWs

YOUR WHATs

Decisions/actions that **were (would be) aligned** with you WHY:	Decisions/actions that **weren't (wouldn't be) aligned** with your WHY:

THE CELERY TEST FOR INDIVIDUALS

Date:_____

YOUR WHY	YOUR HOWs

YOUR WHATs	
Decisions/actions that **were (would be) aligned** with you WHY:	Decisions/actions that **weren't (wouldn't be) aligned** with your WHY:

THE CELERY TEST FOR INDIVIDUALS

Date:_____

YOUR WHY	YOUR HOWs

YOUR WHATs

Decisions/actions that **were (would be) aligned** with you WHY:	Decisions/actions that **weren't (wouldn't be) aligned** with your WHY:

THE CELERY TEST FOR INDIVIDUALS

Date:_____

YOUR WHY	YOUR HOWs

YOUR WHATs

Decisions/actions that **were (would be) aligned** with you WHY:	Decisions/actions that **weren't (wouldn't be) aligned** with your WHY:

THE CELERY TEST FOR INDIVIDUALS

Date:_____

YOUR WHY	YOUR HOWs
_____	_____
_____	_____
_____	_____
_____	_____
_____	_____
_____	_____
_____	_____
_____	_____

YOUR WHATs

Decisions/actions that **were (would be) aligned** with you WHY:	Decisions/actions that **weren't (wouldn't be) aligned** with your WHY:
_____	_____
_____	_____
_____	_____
_____	_____
_____	_____
_____	_____
_____	_____
_____	_____
_____	_____
_____	_____
_____	_____
_____	_____
_____	_____
_____	_____
_____	_____
_____	_____
_____	_____
_____	_____
_____	_____

THE CELERY TEST FOR INDIVIDUALS

Date:_____

YOUR WHY	YOUR HOWs
_____	_____
_____	_____
_____	_____
_____	_____
_____	_____
_____	_____
_____	_____
_____	_____
_____	_____

YOUR WHATs

Decisions/actions that **were (would be) aligned** with you WHY:	Decisions/actions that **weren't (wouldn't be) aligned** with your WHY:
_____	_____
_____	_____
_____	_____
_____	_____
_____	_____
_____	_____
_____	_____
_____	_____
_____	_____
_____	_____
_____	_____
_____	_____
_____	_____
_____	_____
_____	_____
_____	_____
_____	_____
_____	_____
_____	_____

THE CELERY TEST FOR INDIVIDUALS

Date:_____

YOUR WHY	YOUR HOWs
_____	_____
_____	_____
_____	_____
_____	_____
_____	_____
_____	_____
_____	_____
_____	_____

YOUR WHATs

Decisions/actions that **were (would be) aligned** with you WHY:	Decisions/actions that **weren't (wouldn't be) aligned** with your WHY:
_____	_____
_____	_____
_____	_____
_____	_____
_____	_____
_____	_____
_____	_____
_____	_____
_____	_____
_____	_____
_____	_____
_____	_____
_____	_____
_____	_____
_____	_____
_____	_____
_____	_____

Date:_____

YOUR WHY	YOUR HOWs

YOUR WHATs

Decisions/actions that **were (would be) aligned** with you WHY:	Decisions/actions that **weren't (wouldn't be) aligned** with your WHY:

Date:_____

YOUR WHY	YOUR HOWs
_____	_____
_____	_____
_____	_____
_____	_____
_____	_____
_____	_____
_____	_____
_____	_____
_____	_____

YOUR WHATs

Decisions/actions that **were (would be) aligned** with you WHY:	Decisions/actions that **weren't (wouldn't be) aligned** with your WHY:
_____	_____
_____	_____
_____	_____
_____	_____
_____	_____
_____	_____
_____	_____
_____	_____
_____	_____
_____	_____
_____	_____
_____	_____
_____	_____
_____	_____
_____	_____
_____	_____
_____	_____
_____	_____
_____	_____

Date:_____

YOUR WHY	YOUR HOWs
_____	_____
_____	_____
_____	_____
_____	_____
_____	_____
_____	_____
_____	_____
_____	_____
_____	_____

YOUR WHATs

Decisions/actions that **were (would be) aligned** with you WHY:	Decisions/actions that **weren't (wouldn't be) aligned** with your WHY:
_____	_____
_____	_____
_____	_____
_____	_____
_____	_____
_____	_____
_____	_____
_____	_____
_____	_____
_____	_____
_____	_____
_____	_____
_____	_____
_____	_____
_____	_____
_____	_____
_____	_____
_____	_____
_____	_____

THE CELERY TEST FOR INDIVIDUALS

Date:_____

YOUR WHY	YOUR HOWs
_____	_____
_____	_____
_____	_____
_____	_____
_____	_____
_____	_____
_____	_____
_____	_____

YOUR WHATs

Decisions/actions that **were (would be) aligned** with you WHY:	Decisions/actions that **weren't (wouldn't be) aligned** with your WHY:
_____	_____
_____	_____
_____	_____
_____	_____
_____	_____
_____	_____
_____	_____
_____	_____
_____	_____
_____	_____
_____	_____
_____	_____
_____	_____
_____	_____
_____	_____
_____	_____
_____	_____
_____	_____
_____	_____

THE CELERY TEST FOR INDIVIDUALS

Date:_____

YOUR WHY	YOUR HOWs
_____	_____
_____	_____
_____	_____
_____	_____
_____	_____
_____	_____
_____	_____
_____	_____
_____	_____

YOUR WHATs

Decisions/actions that **were (would be) aligned** with you WHY:	Decisions/actions that **weren't (wouldn't be) aligned** with your WHY:
_____	_____
_____	_____
_____	_____
_____	_____
_____	_____
_____	_____
_____	_____
_____	_____
_____	_____
_____	_____
_____	_____
_____	_____
_____	_____
_____	_____
_____	_____
_____	_____
_____	_____
_____	_____
_____	_____

THE CELERY TEST FOR INDIVIDUALS

Date:_____

YOUR WHY	YOUR HOWs
_____	_____
_____	_____
_____	_____
_____	_____
_____	_____
_____	_____
_____	_____
_____	_____

YOUR WHATs

Decisions/actions that **were (would be) aligned** with you WHY:	Decisions/actions that **weren't (wouldn't be) aligned** with your WHY:
_____	_____
_____	_____
_____	_____
_____	_____
_____	_____
_____	_____
_____	_____
_____	_____
_____	_____
_____	_____
_____	_____
_____	_____
_____	_____
_____	_____
_____	_____
_____	_____
_____	_____
_____	_____
_____	_____

THE CELERY TEST FOR INDIVIDUALS

Date:_____

YOUR WHY	YOUR HOWs

YOUR WHATs

Decisions/actions that **were (would be) aligned** with you WHY:	Decisions/actions that **weren't (wouldn't be) aligned** with your WHY:

Date:_____

YOUR WHY	YOUR HOWs

YOUR WHATs

Decisions/actions that **were (would be) aligned** with you WHY:	Decisions/actions that **weren't (wouldn't be) aligned** with your WHY:

THE CELERY TEST FOR INDIVIDUALS

Date:_____

YOUR WHY	YOUR HOWs

YOUR WHATs

Decisions/actions that **were (would be) aligned** with you WHY:	Decisions/actions that **weren't (wouldn't be) aligned** with your WHY:

THE CELERY TEST FOR INDIVIDUALS

Date:_____

YOUR WHY	YOUR HOWs
_____	_____
_____	_____
_____	_____
_____	_____
_____	_____
_____	_____
_____	_____
_____	_____

YOUR WHATs

Decisions/actions that **were (would be) aligned** with you WHY:	Decisions/actions that **weren't (wouldn't be) aligned** with your WHY:
_____	_____
_____	_____
_____	_____
_____	_____
_____	_____
_____	_____
_____	_____
_____	_____
_____	_____
_____	_____
_____	_____
_____	_____
_____	_____
_____	_____
_____	_____
_____	_____
_____	_____
_____	_____
_____	_____

THE CELERY TEST FOR INDIVIDUALS

Date:_____

YOUR WHY	YOUR HOWs

YOUR WHATs

Decisions/actions that **were (would be) aligned** with you WHY:	Decisions/actions that **weren't (wouldn't be) aligned** with your WHY:

THE CELERY TEST FOR INDIVIDUALS

Date:_____

YOUR WHY	YOUR HOWs

YOUR WHATs

Decisions/actions that **were (would be) aligned** with you WHY:	Decisions/actions that **weren't (wouldn't be) aligned** with your WHY:

THE CELERY TEST FOR INDIVIDUALS

Date:_____

YOUR WHY	YOUR HOWs

YOUR WHATs

Decisions/actions that **were (would be) aligned** with you WHY:	Decisions/actions that **weren't (wouldn't be) aligned** with your WHY:

THE CELERY TEST FOR INDIVIDUALS

Date:_____

YOUR WHY	YOUR HOWs
_____	_____
_____	_____
_____	_____
_____	_____
_____	_____
_____	_____
_____	_____
_____	_____

YOUR WHATs

Decisions/actions that **were (would be) aligned** with you WHY:	Decisions/actions that **weren't (wouldn't be) aligned** with your WHY:
_____	_____
_____	_____
_____	_____
_____	_____
_____	_____
_____	_____
_____	_____
_____	_____
_____	_____
_____	_____
_____	_____
_____	_____
_____	_____
_____	_____
_____	_____
_____	_____
_____	_____
_____	_____
_____	_____

THE CELERY TEST FOR INDIVIDUALS

Date:_____

YOUR WHY	YOUR HOWs

Decisions/actions that **were (would be) aligned** with you WHY:	Decisions/actions that **weren't (wouldn't be) aligned** with your WHY:

YOUR WHATs

THE CELERY TEST FOR INDIVIDUALS

Date:_____

YOUR WHY	YOUR HOWs
_____	_____
_____	_____
_____	_____
_____	_____
_____	_____
_____	_____
_____	_____
_____	_____
_____	_____

YOUR WHATs

Decisions/actions that **were (would be) aligned** with you WHY:	Decisions/actions that **weren't (wouldn't be) aligned** with your WHY:
_____	_____
_____	_____
_____	_____
_____	_____
_____	_____
_____	_____
_____	_____
_____	_____
_____	_____
_____	_____
_____	_____
_____	_____
_____	_____
_____	_____
_____	_____
_____	_____
_____	_____
_____	_____

Date:_____

YOUR WHY	YOUR HOWs

YOUR WHATs

Decisions/actions that **were (would be) aligned** with you WHY:	Decisions/actions that **weren't (wouldn't be) aligned** with your WHY:

THE CELERY TEST FOR INDIVIDUALS

Date:_____

YOUR WHY	YOUR HOWs
_____	_____
_____	_____
_____	_____
_____	_____
_____	_____
_____	_____
_____	_____
_____	_____

YOUR WHATs

Decisions/actions that **were (would be) aligned** with you WHY:	Decisions/actions that **weren't (wouldn't be) aligned** with your WHY:
_____	_____
_____	_____
_____	_____
_____	_____
_____	_____
_____	_____
_____	_____
_____	_____
_____	_____
_____	_____
_____	_____
_____	_____
_____	_____
_____	_____
_____	_____
_____	_____
_____	_____
_____	_____
_____	_____
_____	_____

THE CELERY TEST FOR INDIVIDUALS

Date:_____

YOUR WHY	YOUR HOWs

YOUR WHATs

Decisions/actions that **were (would be) aligned** with you WHY:	Decisions/actions that **weren't (wouldn't be) aligned** with your WHY:

THE CELERY TEST FOR INDIVIDUALS

Date:_____

YOUR WHY	YOUR HOWs

YOUR WHATs

Decisions/actions that **were (would be) aligned** with you WHY:	Decisions/actions that **weren't (wouldn't be) aligned** with your WHY:

THE CELERY TEST FOR INDIVIDUALS

Date:_____

YOUR WHY	YOUR HOWs
_____	_____
_____	_____
_____	_____
_____	_____
_____	_____
_____	_____
_____	_____
_____	_____
_____	_____

YOUR WHATs

Decisions/actions that **were (would be) aligned** with you WHY:	Decisions/actions that **weren't (wouldn't be) aligned** with your WHY:
_____	_____
_____	_____
_____	_____
_____	_____
_____	_____
_____	_____
_____	_____
_____	_____
_____	_____
_____	_____
_____	_____
_____	_____
_____	_____
_____	_____
_____	_____
_____	_____
_____	_____
_____	_____
_____	_____
_____	_____

THE CELERY TEST FOR INDIVIDUALS

Date:_____

YOUR WHY	YOUR HOWs
_____	_____
_____	_____
_____	_____
_____	_____
_____	_____
_____	_____
_____	_____
_____	_____
_____	_____

YOUR WHATs

Decisions/actions that **were (would be) aligned** with you WHY:	Decisions/actions that **weren't (wouldn't be) aligned** with your WHY:

Date:_____

YOUR WHY	YOUR HOWs
_____	_____
_____	_____
_____	_____
_____	_____
_____	_____
_____	_____
_____	_____
_____	_____
_____	_____

YOUR WHATs	
Decisions/actions that **were (would be) aligned** with you WHY:	Decisions/actions that **weren't (wouldn't be) aligned** with your WHY:
_____	_____
_____	_____
_____	_____
_____	_____
_____	_____
_____	_____
_____	_____
_____	_____
_____	_____
_____	_____
_____	_____
_____	_____
_____	_____
_____	_____
_____	_____
_____	_____
_____	_____
_____	_____
_____	_____
_____	_____

Date:_____

YOUR WHY	YOUR HOWs
_____	_____
_____	_____
_____	_____
_____	_____
_____	_____
_____	_____
_____	_____
_____	_____

YOUR WHATs

Decisions/actions that **were (would be) aligned** with you WHY:	Decisions/actions that **weren't (wouldn't be) aligned** with your WHY:
_____	_____
_____	_____
_____	_____
_____	_____
_____	_____
_____	_____
_____	_____
_____	_____
_____	_____
_____	_____
_____	_____
_____	_____
_____	_____
_____	_____
_____	_____
_____	_____
_____	_____
_____	_____

THE CELERY TEST FOR INDIVIDUALS

Date:_____

YOUR WHY	YOUR HOWs

YOUR WHATs

Decisions/actions that **were (would be) aligned** with you WHY:	Decisions/actions that **weren't (wouldn't be) aligned** with your WHY:

THE CELERY TEST FOR INDIVIDUALS

Date:_____

YOUR WHY	YOUR HOWs
_____	_____
_____	_____
_____	_____
_____	_____
_____	_____
_____	_____
_____	_____
_____	_____
_____	_____

YOUR WHATs

Decisions/actions that **were (would be) aligned** with you WHY:	Decisions/actions that **weren't (wouldn't be) aligned** with your WHY:
_____	_____
_____	_____
_____	_____
_____	_____
_____	_____
_____	_____
_____	_____
_____	_____
_____	_____
_____	_____
_____	_____
_____	_____
_____	_____
_____	_____
_____	_____
_____	_____
_____	_____
_____	_____
_____	_____

Date:_____

YOUR WHY	YOUR HOWs

YOUR WHATs

Decisions/actions that **were (would be) aligned** with you WHY:	Decisions/actions that **weren't (wouldn't be) aligned** with your WHY:

THE CELERY TEST FOR INDIVIDUALS

Date:_____

YOUR WHY	YOUR HOWs
_____	_____
_____	_____
_____	_____
_____	_____
_____	_____
_____	_____
_____	_____
_____	_____

YOUR WHATs

Decisions/actions that **were (would be) aligned** with you WHY:	Decisions/actions that **weren't (wouldn't be) aligned** with your WHY:
_____	_____
_____	_____
_____	_____
_____	_____
_____	_____
_____	_____
_____	_____
_____	_____
_____	_____
_____	_____
_____	_____
_____	_____
_____	_____
_____	_____
_____	_____
_____	_____
_____	_____

THE CELERY TEST FOR INDIVIDUALS

Date:_____

YOUR WHY	YOUR HOWs

YOUR WHATs

Decisions/actions that **were (would be) aligned** with you WHY:	Decisions/actions that **weren't (wouldn't be) aligned** with your WHY:

THE CELERY TEST FOR INDIVIDUALS

Date:_____

YOUR WHY	YOUR HOWs
_____	_____
_____	_____
_____	_____
_____	_____
_____	_____
_____	_____
_____	_____
_____	_____

YOUR WHATs

Decisions/actions that **were (would be) aligned** with you WHY:	Decisions/actions that **weren't (wouldn't be) aligned** with your WHY:
_____	_____
_____	_____
_____	_____
_____	_____
_____	_____
_____	_____
_____	_____
_____	_____
_____	_____
_____	_____
_____	_____
_____	_____
_____	_____
_____	_____
_____	_____
_____	_____
_____	_____
_____	_____
_____	_____

THE CELERY TEST FOR INDIVIDUALS

Date:_____

YOUR WHY	YOUR HOWs
_____	_____
_____	_____
_____	_____
_____	_____
_____	_____
_____	_____
_____	_____
_____	_____

YOUR WHATs

Decisions/actions that **were (would be) aligned** with you WHY:	Decisions/actions that **weren't (wouldn't be) aligned** with your WHY:
_____	_____
_____	_____
_____	_____
_____	_____
_____	_____
_____	_____
_____	_____
_____	_____
_____	_____
_____	_____
_____	_____
_____	_____
_____	_____
_____	_____
_____	_____
_____	_____
_____	_____
_____	_____
_____	_____
_____	_____

THE CELERY TEST FOR INDIVIDUALS

Date:_____

YOUR WHY	YOUR HOWs
_____	_____
_____	_____
_____	_____
_____	_____
_____	_____
_____	_____
_____	_____
_____	_____

YOUR WHATs

Decisions/actions that **were (would be) aligned** with you WHY:	Decisions/actions that **weren't (wouldn't be) aligned** with your WHY:
_____	_____
_____	_____
_____	_____
_____	_____
_____	_____
_____	_____
_____	_____
_____	_____
_____	_____
_____	_____
_____	_____
_____	_____
_____	_____
_____	_____
_____	_____
_____	_____
_____	_____
_____	_____
_____	_____
_____	_____

Date:_____

YOUR WHY	YOUR HOWs

YOUR WHATs

Decisions/actions that **were (would be) aligned** with you WHY:	Decisions/actions that **weren't (wouldn't be) aligned** with your WHY:

THE CELERY TEST FOR INDIVIDUALS

Date:_____

YOUR WHY	YOUR HOWs

_____

YOUR WHATs

Decisions/actions that **were (would be) aligned** with you WHY:	Decisions/actions that **weren't (wouldn't be) aligned** with your WHY:

Date:_____

YOUR WHY	YOUR HOWs

YOUR WHATs

Decisions/actions that **were (would be) aligned** with you WHY:	Decisions/actions that **weren't (wouldn't be) aligned** with your WHY:

Date:_____

YOUR WHY	YOUR HOWs
_____	_____
_____	_____
_____	_____
_____	_____
_____	_____
_____	_____
_____	_____
_____	_____

YOUR WHATs	
Decisions/actions that **were (would be) aligned** with you WHY:	Decisions/actions that **weren't (wouldn't be) aligned** with your WHY:
_____	_____
_____	_____
_____	_____
_____	_____
_____	_____
_____	_____
_____	_____
_____	_____
_____	_____
_____	_____
_____	_____
_____	_____
_____	_____
_____	_____
_____	_____
_____	_____
_____	_____
_____	_____

THE CELERY TEST FOR INDIVIDUALS

Date:_____

YOUR WHY	YOUR HOWs

YOUR WHATs

Decisions/actions that **were (would be) aligned** with you WHY:	Decisions/actions that **weren't (wouldn't be) aligned** with your WHY:

THE CELERY TEST FOR INDIVIDUALS

Date:_____

YOUR WHY	YOUR HOWs

YOUR WHATs

Decisions/actions that **were (would be) aligned** with you WHY:	Decisions/actions that **weren't (wouldn't be) aligned** with your WHY:

Date:_____

YOUR WHY	YOUR HOWs
_____	_____
_____	_____
_____	_____
_____	_____
_____	_____
_____	_____
_____	_____
_____	_____

YOUR WHATs

Decisions/actions that **were (would be) aligned** with you WHY:	Decisions/actions that **weren't (wouldn't be) aligned** with your WHY:
_____	_____
_____	_____
_____	_____
_____	_____
_____	_____
_____	_____
_____	_____
_____	_____
_____	_____
_____	_____
_____	_____
_____	_____
_____	_____
_____	_____
_____	_____
_____	_____
_____	_____
_____	_____
_____	_____
_____	_____

THE CELERY TEST FOR INDIVIDUALS

Date:_____

YOUR WHY	YOUR HOWs
_____	_____
_____	_____
_____	_____
_____	_____
_____	_____
_____	_____
_____	_____
_____	_____

YOUR WHATs

Decisions/actions that **were (would be) aligned** with you WHY:	Decisions/actions that **weren't (wouldn't be) aligned** with your WHY:
_____	_____
_____	_____
_____	_____
_____	_____
_____	_____
_____	_____
_____	_____
_____	_____
_____	_____
_____	_____
_____	_____
_____	_____
_____	_____
_____	_____
_____	_____
_____	_____
_____	_____
_____	_____

THE CELERY TEST FOR INDIVIDUALS

Date:_____

YOUR WHY	YOUR HOWs
_____	_____
_____	_____
_____	_____
_____	_____
_____	_____
_____	_____
_____	_____
_____	_____
_____	_____

YOUR WHATs

Decisions/actions that **were (would be) aligned** with you WHY:	Decisions/actions that **weren't (wouldn't be) aligned** with your WHY:
_____	_____
_____	_____
_____	_____
_____	_____
_____	_____
_____	_____
_____	_____
_____	_____
_____	_____
_____	_____
_____	_____
_____	_____
_____	_____
_____	_____
_____	_____
_____	_____
_____	_____
_____	_____
_____	_____

Date:_____

YOUR WHY	YOUR HOWs

YOUR WHATs

Decisions/actions that **were (would be) aligned** with you WHY:	Decisions/actions that **weren't (wouldn't be) aligned** with your WHY:

Date:_____

YOUR WHY	YOUR HOWs

YOUR WHATs

Decisions/actions that **were (would be) aligned** with you WHY:	Decisions/actions that **weren't (wouldn't be) aligned** with your WHY:

THE CELERY TEST FOR INDIVIDUALS

Date:_____

YOUR WHY	YOUR HOWs
_____	_____
_____	_____
_____	_____
_____	_____
_____	_____
_____	_____
_____	_____
_____	_____
_____	_____

YOUR WHATs

Decisions/actions that **were (would be) aligned** with you WHY:	Decisions/actions that **weren't (wouldn't be) aligned** with your WHY:
_____	_____
_____	_____
_____	_____
_____	_____
_____	_____
_____	_____
_____	_____
_____	_____
_____	_____
_____	_____
_____	_____
_____	_____
_____	_____
_____	_____
_____	_____
_____	_____
_____	_____
_____	_____
_____	_____

Date:_____

YOUR WHY	YOUR HOWs

YOUR WHATs

Decisions/actions that **were (would be) aligned** with you WHY:	Decisions/actions that **weren't (wouldn't be) aligned** with your WHY:

Date:_____

YOUR WHY	YOUR HOWs

YOUR WHATs

Decisions/actions that **were (would be) aligned** with you WHY:	Decisions/actions that **weren't (wouldn't be) aligned** with your WHY:

THE CELERY TEST FOR INDIVIDUALS

Date:_____

YOUR WHY	YOUR HOWs
_____	_____
_____	_____
_____	_____
_____	_____
_____	_____
_____	_____
_____	_____
_____	_____

YOUR WHATs

Decisions/actions that **were (would be) aligned** with you WHY:	Decisions/actions that **weren't (wouldn't be) aligned** with your WHY:

THE CELERY TEST FOR INDIVIDUALS

Date:_____

YOUR WHY	YOUR HOWs
_____	_____
_____	_____
_____	_____
_____	_____
_____	_____
_____	_____
_____	_____

YOUR WHATs

Decisions/actions that **were (would be) aligned** with you WHY:	Decisions/actions that **weren't (wouldn't be) aligned** with your WHY:

Date:_____

YOUR WHY	YOUR HOWs
_____	_____
_____	_____
_____	_____
_____	_____
_____	_____
_____	_____
_____	_____
_____	_____
_____	_____

YOUR WHATs

Decisions/actions that **were (would be) aligned** with you WHY:	Decisions/actions that **weren't (wouldn't be) aligned** with your WHY:
_____	_____
_____	_____
_____	_____
_____	_____
_____	_____
_____	_____
_____	_____
_____	_____
_____	_____
_____	_____
_____	_____
_____	_____
_____	_____
_____	_____
_____	_____
_____	_____
_____	_____
_____	_____
_____	_____
_____	_____

Date:_____

YOUR WHY	YOUR HOWs

YOUR WHATs

Decisions/actions that **were (would be) aligned** with you WHY:	Decisions/actions that **weren't (wouldn't be) aligned** with your WHY:

Date:_____

YOUR WHY	YOUR HOWs
_____	_____
_____	_____
_____	_____
_____	_____
_____	_____
_____	_____
_____	_____
_____	_____

YOUR WHATs

Decisions/actions that **were (would be) aligned** with you WHY:	Decisions/actions that **weren't (wouldn't be) aligned** with your WHY:
_____	_____
_____	_____
_____	_____
_____	_____
_____	_____
_____	_____
_____	_____
_____	_____
_____	_____
_____	_____
_____	_____
_____	_____
_____	_____
_____	_____
_____	_____
_____	_____
_____	_____
_____	_____

THE CELERY TEST FOR INDIVIDUALS

Date:_____

YOUR WHY	YOUR HOWs
_____	_____
_____	_____
_____	_____
_____	_____
_____	_____
_____	_____
_____	_____
_____	_____

YOUR WHATs

Decisions/actions that **were (would be) aligned** with you WHY:	Decisions/actions that **weren't (wouldn't be) aligned** with your WHY:
_____	_____
_____	_____
_____	_____
_____	_____
_____	_____
_____	_____
_____	_____
_____	_____
_____	_____
_____	_____
_____	_____
_____	_____
_____	_____
_____	_____
_____	_____
_____	_____
_____	_____

THE CELERY TEST FOR INDIVIDUALS

Date:_____

YOUR WHY	YOUR HOWs
_____	_____
_____	_____
_____	_____
_____	_____
_____	_____
_____	_____
_____	_____
_____	_____

YOUR WHATs

Decisions/actions that **were (would be) aligned** with you WHY:	Decisions/actions that **weren't (wouldn't be) aligned** with your WHY:
_____	_____
_____	_____
_____	_____
_____	_____
_____	_____
_____	_____
_____	_____
_____	_____
_____	_____
_____	_____
_____	_____
_____	_____
_____	_____
_____	_____
_____	_____
_____	_____
_____	_____
_____	_____

Date:_____

YOUR WHY	YOUR HOWs

YOUR WHATs

Decisions/actions that **were (would be) aligned** with you WHY:	Decisions/actions that **weren't (wouldn't be) aligned** with your WHY:

THE CELERY TEST FOR INDIVIDUALS

Date:_____

YOUR WHY	YOUR HOWs
_____	_____
_____	_____
_____	_____
_____	_____
_____	_____
_____	_____
_____	_____
_____	_____

YOUR WHATs

Decisions/actions that **were (would be) aligned** with you WHY:	Decisions/actions that **weren't (wouldn't be) aligned** with your WHY:
_____	_____
_____	_____
_____	_____
_____	_____
_____	_____
_____	_____
_____	_____
_____	_____
_____	_____
_____	_____
_____	_____
_____	_____
_____	_____
_____	_____
_____	_____
_____	_____
_____	_____
_____	_____

THE CELERY TEST FOR INDIVIDUALS

Date:_____

YOUR WHY	YOUR HOWs
_____	_____
_____	_____
_____	_____
_____	_____
_____	_____
_____	_____
_____	_____

YOUR WHATs

Decisions/actions that **were (would be) aligned** with you WHY:	Decisions/actions that **weren't (wouldn't be) aligned** with your WHY:
_____	_____
_____	_____
_____	_____
_____	_____
_____	_____
_____	_____
_____	_____
_____	_____
_____	_____
_____	_____
_____	_____
_____	_____
_____	_____
_____	_____
_____	_____
_____	_____
_____	_____

THE CELERY TEST FOR INDIVIDUALS

Date:_____

YOUR WHY	YOUR HOWs

YOUR WHATs

Decisions/actions that **were (would be) aligned** with you WHY:	Decisions/actions that **weren't (wouldn't be) aligned** with your WHY:

THE CELERY TEST FOR INDIVIDUALS

Date:_____

YOUR WHY	YOUR HOWs
_____	_____
_____	_____
_____	_____
_____	_____
_____	_____
_____	_____
_____	_____
_____	_____

YOUR WHATs	
Decisions/actions that **were (would be) aligned** with you WHY:	Decisions/actions that **weren't (wouldn't be) aligned** with your WHY:
_____	_____
_____	_____
_____	_____
_____	_____
_____	_____
_____	_____
_____	_____
_____	_____
_____	_____
_____	_____
_____	_____
_____	_____
_____	_____
_____	_____
_____	_____
_____	_____
_____	_____
_____	_____

THE CELERY TEST FOR INDIVIDUALS

Date:_____

YOUR WHY	YOUR HOWs

YOUR WHATs

Decisions/actions that **were (would be) aligned** with you WHY:	Decisions/actions that **weren't (wouldn't be) aligned** with your WHY:

Date:_____

YOUR WHY	YOUR HOWs
_____	_____
_____	_____
_____	_____
_____	_____
_____	_____
_____	_____
_____	_____
_____	_____

YOUR WHATs

Decisions/actions that **were (would be) aligned** with you WHY:	Decisions/actions that **weren't (wouldn't be) aligned** with your WHY:

THE CELERY TEST FOR INDIVIDUALS

Date:_____

YOUR WHY	YOUR HOWs
_____	_____
_____	_____
_____	_____
_____	_____
_____	_____
_____	_____
_____	_____
_____	_____
_____	_____

YOUR WHATs

Decisions/actions that **were (would be) aligned** with you WHY:	Decisions/actions that **weren't (wouldn't be) aligned** with your WHY:
_____	_____
_____	_____
_____	_____
_____	_____
_____	_____
_____	_____
_____	_____
_____	_____
_____	_____
_____	_____
_____	_____
_____	_____
_____	_____
_____	_____
_____	_____
_____	_____
_____	_____
_____	_____
_____	_____
_____	_____

THE CELERY TEST FOR INDIVIDUALS

Date:_____

YOUR WHY	YOUR HOWs
_____	_____
_____	_____
_____	_____
_____	_____
_____	_____
_____	_____
_____	_____
_____	_____

YOUR WHATs

Decisions/actions that **were (would be) aligned** with you WHY:	Decisions/actions that **weren't (wouldn't be) aligned** with your WHY:

Date:_____

YOUR WHY	YOUR HOWs
_____	_____
_____	_____
_____	_____
_____	_____
_____	_____
_____	_____
_____	_____
_____	_____

YOUR WHATs

Decisions/actions that **were (would be) aligned** with you WHY:	Decisions/actions that **weren't (wouldn't be) aligned** with your WHY:
_____	_____
_____	_____
_____	_____
_____	_____
_____	_____
_____	_____
_____	_____
_____	_____
_____	_____
_____	_____
_____	_____
_____	_____
_____	_____
_____	_____
_____	_____
_____	_____
_____	_____
_____	_____
_____	_____
_____	_____

Date:_____

YOUR WHY	YOUR HOWs
_____	_____
_____	_____
_____	_____
_____	_____
_____	_____
_____	_____
_____	_____

YOUR WHATs

Decisions/actions that **were (would be) aligned** with you WHY:	Decisions/actions that **weren't (wouldn't be) aligned** with your WHY:
_____	_____
_____	_____
_____	_____
_____	_____
_____	_____
_____	_____
_____	_____
_____	_____
_____	_____
_____	_____
_____	_____
_____	_____
_____	_____
_____	_____
_____	_____
_____	_____

THE CELERY TEST FOR INDIVIDUALS

Date:_____

YOUR WHY	YOUR HOWs

YOUR WHATs

Decisions/actions that **were (would be) aligned** with you WHY:	Decisions/actions that **weren't (wouldn't be) aligned** with your WHY:

THE CELERY TEST FOR INDIVIDUALS

Date:_____

YOUR WHY	YOUR HOWs

YOUR WHATs

Decisions/actions that **were (would be) aligned** with you WHY:	Decisions/actions that **weren't (wouldn't be) aligned** with your WHY:

THE CELERY TEST FOR INDIVIDUALS

Date:_____

YOUR WHY	YOUR HOWs

YOUR WHATs

Decisions/actions that **were (would be) aligned** with you WHY:	Decisions/actions that **weren't (wouldn't be) aligned** with your WHY:

THE CELERY TEST FOR INDIVIDUALS

Date:_____

YOUR WHY	YOUR HOWs
_____	_____
_____	_____
_____	_____
_____	_____
_____	_____
_____	_____
_____	_____
_____	_____

YOUR WHATs

Decisions/actions that **were (would be) aligned** with you WHY:	Decisions/actions that **weren't (wouldn't be) aligned** with your WHY:
_____	_____
_____	_____
_____	_____
_____	_____
_____	_____
_____	_____
_____	_____
_____	_____
_____	_____
_____	_____
_____	_____
_____	_____
_____	_____
_____	_____
_____	_____
_____	_____
_____	_____
_____	_____

THE CELERY TEST FOR INDIVIDUALS

Date:_____

YOUR WHY	YOUR HOWs

YOUR WHATs

Decisions/actions that **were (would be) aligned** with you WHY:	Decisions/actions that **weren't (wouldn't be) aligned** with your WHY:

Date:_____

YOUR WHY	YOUR HOWs

YOUR WHATs

Decisions/actions that **were (would be) aligned** with you WHY:	Decisions/actions that **weren't (wouldn't be) aligned** with your WHY:

THE CELERY TEST FOR INDIVIDUALS

Date:_____

YOUR WHY	YOUR HOWs
_____	_____
_____	_____
_____	_____
_____	_____
_____	_____
_____	_____
_____	_____
_____	_____

YOUR WHATs

Decisions/actions that **were (would be) aligned** with you WHY:	Decisions/actions that **weren't (wouldn't be) aligned** with your WHY:
_____	_____
_____	_____
_____	_____
_____	_____
_____	_____
_____	_____
_____	_____
_____	_____
_____	_____
_____	_____
_____	_____
_____	_____
_____	_____
_____	_____
_____	_____
_____	_____
_____	_____
_____	_____
_____	_____

THE CELERY TEST FOR INDIVIDUALS

Date:_____

YOUR WHY

_____
_____
_____
_____
_____
_____
_____
_____

YOUR HOWs

_____
_____
_____
_____
_____
_____
_____
_____

YOUR WHATs

Decisions/actions that **were (would be) aligned** with you WHY:	Decisions/actions that **weren't (wouldn't be) aligned** with your WHY:

Date:_____

YOUR WHY	YOUR HOWs
_____	_____
_____	_____
_____	_____
_____	_____
_____	_____
_____	_____
_____	_____
_____	_____
_____	_____

YOUR WHATs

Decisions/actions that **were (would be) aligned** with you WHY:	Decisions/actions that **weren't (wouldn't be) aligned** with your WHY:

THE CELERY TEST FOR INDIVIDUALS

Date:_____

YOUR WHY	YOUR HOWs
_____	_____
_____	_____
_____	_____
_____	_____
_____	_____
_____	_____
_____	_____
_____	_____

YOUR WHATs

Decisions/actions that **were (would be) aligned** with you WHY:	Decisions/actions that **weren't (wouldn't be) aligned** with your WHY:
_____	_____
_____	_____
_____	_____
_____	_____
_____	_____
_____	_____
_____	_____
_____	_____
_____	_____
_____	_____
_____	_____
_____	_____
_____	_____
_____	_____
_____	_____
_____	_____
_____	_____
_____	_____
_____	_____
_____	_____

THE CELERY TEST FOR INDIVIDUALS

Date:_____

YOUR WHY	YOUR HOWs

YOUR WHATs

Decisions/actions that **were (would be) aligned** with you WHY:	Decisions/actions that **weren't (wouldn't be) aligned** with your WHY:

Date:_____

YOUR WHY	YOUR HOWs
_____	_____
_____	_____
_____	_____
_____	_____
_____	_____
_____	_____
_____	_____
_____	_____

YOUR WHATs

Decisions/actions that **were (would be) aligned** with you WHY:	Decisions/actions that **weren't (wouldn't be) aligned** with your WHY:
_____	_____
_____	_____
_____	_____
_____	_____
_____	_____
_____	_____
_____	_____
_____	_____
_____	_____
_____	_____
_____	_____
_____	_____
_____	_____
_____	_____
_____	_____
_____	_____
_____	_____
_____	_____
_____	_____

THE CELERY TEST FOR INDIVIDUALS

Date:_____

YOUR WHY	YOUR HOWs

YOUR WHATs

Decisions/actions that **were (would be) aligned** with you WHY:	Decisions/actions that **weren't (wouldn't be) aligned** with your WHY:

THE CELERY TEST FOR INDIVIDUALS

Date:_____

YOUR WHY	YOUR HOWs

YOUR WHATs

Decisions/actions that **were (would be) aligned** with you WHY:	Decisions/actions that **weren't (wouldn't be) aligned** with your WHY:

Date:_____

YOUR WHY	YOUR HOWs

YOUR WHATs

Decisions/actions that **were (would be) aligned** with you WHY:	Decisions/actions that **weren't (wouldn't be) aligned** with your WHY:

Date:_____

YOUR WHY	YOUR HOWs
_____	_____
_____	_____
_____	_____
_____	_____
_____	_____
_____	_____
_____	_____
_____	_____

YOUR WHATs

Decisions/actions that **were (would be) aligned** with you WHY:	Decisions/actions that **weren't (wouldn't be) aligned** with your WHY:

THE CELERY TEST FOR INDIVIDUALS

Date:_____

YOUR WHY	YOUR HOWs

YOUR WHATs

Decisions/actions that **were (would be) aligned** with you WHY:	Decisions/actions that **weren't (wouldn't be) aligned** with your WHY:

THE CELERY TEST FOR INDIVIDUALS

Date:_____

YOUR WHY	YOUR HOWs

YOUR WHATs

Decisions/actions that **were (would be) aligned** with you WHY:	Decisions/actions that **weren't (wouldn't be) aligned** with your WHY:

Date:_____

YOUR WHY	YOUR HOWs

YOUR WHATs	
Decisions/actions that **were (would be) aligned** with you WHY:	Decisions/actions that **weren't (wouldn't be) aligned** with your WHY:

THE CELERY TEST FOR INDIVIDUALS

Date:_____

YOUR WHY	YOUR HOWs
_____	_____
_____	_____
_____	_____
_____	_____
_____	_____
_____	_____
_____	_____
_____	_____
_____	_____

YOUR WHATs

Decisions/actions that **were (would be) aligned** with you WHY:	Decisions/actions that **weren't (wouldn't be) aligned** with your WHY:
_____	_____
_____	_____
_____	_____
_____	_____
_____	_____
_____	_____
_____	_____
_____	_____
_____	_____
_____	_____
_____	_____
_____	_____
_____	_____
_____	_____
_____	_____
_____	_____
_____	_____
_____	_____
_____	_____

THE CELERY TEST FOR INDIVIDUALS

Date:_____

YOUR WHY	YOUR HOWs

YOUR WHATs

Decisions/actions that **were (would be) aligned** with you WHY:	Decisions/actions that **weren't (wouldn't be) aligned** with your WHY:

THE CELERY TEST FOR INDIVIDUALS

Date:_____

YOUR WHY	YOUR HOWs

YOUR WHATs

Decisions/actions that **were (would be) aligned** with you WHY:	Decisions/actions that **weren't (wouldn't be) aligned** with your WHY:

Date:_____

YOUR WHY	YOUR HOWs

YOUR WHATs

Decisions/actions that **were (would be) aligned** with you WHY:	Decisions/actions that **weren't (wouldn't be) aligned** with your WHY:

THE CELERY TEST FOR INDIVIDUALS

Date:_____

YOUR WHY	YOUR HOWs

YOUR WHATs

Decisions/actions that **were (would be) aligned** with you WHY:	Decisions/actions that **weren't (wouldn't be) aligned** with your WHY:

THE CELERY TEST FOR INDIVIDUALS

Date:_____

YOUR WHY	YOUR HOWs
_____	_____
_____	_____
_____	_____
_____	_____
_____	_____
_____	_____
_____	_____
_____	_____

YOUR WHATs

Decisions/actions that **were (would be) aligned** with you WHY:	Decisions/actions that **weren't (wouldn't be) aligned** with your WHY:
_____	_____
_____	_____
_____	_____
_____	_____
_____	_____
_____	_____
_____	_____
_____	_____
_____	_____
_____	_____
_____	_____
_____	_____
_____	_____
_____	_____
_____	_____
_____	_____
_____	_____
_____	_____

THE CELERY TEST FOR INDIVIDUALS

Date:_____

YOUR WHY	YOUR HOWs
_____	_____
_____	_____
_____	_____
_____	_____
_____	_____
_____	_____
_____	_____
_____	_____

YOUR WHATs

Decisions/actions that **were (would be) aligned** with you WHY:	Decisions/actions that **weren't (wouldn't be) aligned** with your WHY:

THE CELERY TEST FOR INDIVIDUALS

Date:_____

YOUR WHY	YOUR HOWs
_____	_____
_____	_____
_____	_____
_____	_____
_____	_____
_____	_____
_____	_____
_____	_____

YOUR WHATs

Decisions/actions that **were (would be) aligned** with you WHY:	Decisions/actions that **weren't (wouldn't be) aligned** with your WHY:

Date:_____

YOUR WHY	YOUR HOWs

YOUR WHATs

Decisions/actions that **were (would be) aligned** with you WHY:	Decisions/actions that **weren't (wouldn't be) aligned** with your WHY:

THE CELERY TEST FOR INDIVIDUALS

Date:_____

YOUR WHY	YOUR HOWs
_____	_____
_____	_____
_____	_____
_____	_____
_____	_____
_____	_____
_____	_____
_____	_____
_____	_____

YOUR WHATs

Decisions/actions that **were (would be) aligned** with you WHY:	Decisions/actions that **weren't (wouldn't be) aligned** with your WHY:
_____	_____
_____	_____
_____	_____
_____	_____
_____	_____
_____	_____
_____	_____
_____	_____
_____	_____
_____	_____
_____	_____
_____	_____
_____	_____
_____	_____
_____	_____
_____	_____
_____	_____

THE CELERY TEST FOR INDIVIDUALS

Date:_____

YOUR WHY	YOUR HOWs
_____	_____
_____	_____
_____	_____
_____	_____
_____	_____
_____	_____
_____	_____
_____	_____

YOUR WHATs

Decisions/actions that **were (would be) aligned** with you WHY:	Decisions/actions that **weren't (wouldn't be) aligned** with your WHY:
_____	_____
_____	_____
_____	_____
_____	_____
_____	_____
_____	_____
_____	_____
_____	_____
_____	_____
_____	_____
_____	_____
_____	_____
_____	_____
_____	_____
_____	_____
_____	_____
_____	_____
_____	_____
_____	_____

Date:_____

YOUR WHY	YOUR HOWs
_____	_____
_____	_____
_____	_____
_____	_____
_____	_____
_____	_____
_____	_____
_____	_____
_____	_____

YOUR WHATs	
Decisions/actions that **were (would be) aligned** with you WHY:	Decisions/actions that **weren't (wouldn't be) aligned** with your WHY:
_____	_____
_____	_____
_____	_____
_____	_____
_____	_____
_____	_____
_____	_____
_____	_____
_____	_____
_____	_____
_____	_____
_____	_____
_____	_____
_____	_____
_____	_____
_____	_____
_____	_____
_____	_____
_____	_____
_____	_____

THE CELERY TEST FOR INDIVIDUALS

Date:_____

YOUR WHY	YOUR HOWs
_____	_____
_____	_____
_____	_____
_____	_____
_____	_____
_____	_____
_____	_____
_____	_____

YOUR WHATs

Decisions/actions that **were (would be) aligned** with you WHY:	Decisions/actions that **weren't (wouldn't be) aligned** with your WHY:
_____	_____
_____	_____
_____	_____
_____	_____
_____	_____
_____	_____
_____	_____
_____	_____
_____	_____
_____	_____
_____	_____
_____	_____
_____	_____
_____	_____
_____	_____
_____	_____
_____	_____

Date:_____

YOUR WHY	YOUR HOWs

YOUR WHATs

Decisions/actions that **were (would be) aligned** with you WHY:	Decisions/actions that **weren't (wouldn't be) aligned** with your WHY:

THE CELERY TEST FOR INDIVIDUALS

Date:_____

YOUR WHY	YOUR HOWs
_____	_____
_____	_____
_____	_____
_____	_____
_____	_____
_____	_____
_____	_____
_____	_____

YOUR WHATs

Decisions/actions that **were (would be) aligned** with you WHY:	Decisions/actions that **weren't (wouldn't be) aligned** with your WHY:

THE CELERY TEST FOR INDIVIDUALS

Date:_____

YOUR WHY	YOUR HOWs
_____	_____
_____	_____
_____	_____
_____	_____
_____	_____
_____	_____
_____	_____
_____	_____

YOUR WHATs

Decisions/actions that **were (would be) aligned** with you WHY:	Decisions/actions that **weren't (wouldn't be) aligned** with your WHY:
_____	_____
_____	_____
_____	_____
_____	_____
_____	_____
_____	_____
_____	_____
_____	_____
_____	_____
_____	_____
_____	_____
_____	_____
_____	_____
_____	_____
_____	_____
_____	_____
_____	_____
_____	_____
_____	_____
_____	_____
_____	_____

THE CELERY TEST FOR INDIVIDUALS

Date:_____

YOUR WHY	YOUR HOWs
_____	_____
_____	_____
_____	_____
_____	_____
_____	_____
_____	_____
_____	_____
_____	_____
_____	_____

YOUR WHATs

Decisions/actions that **were (would be) aligned** with you WHY:	Decisions/actions that **weren't (wouldn't be) aligned** with your WHY:
_____	_____
_____	_____
_____	_____
_____	_____
_____	_____
_____	_____
_____	_____
_____	_____
_____	_____
_____	_____
_____	_____
_____	_____
_____	_____
_____	_____
_____	_____
_____	_____
_____	_____
_____	_____
_____	_____
_____	_____

Made in the USA
Monee, IL
09 November 2023

46146311R00083